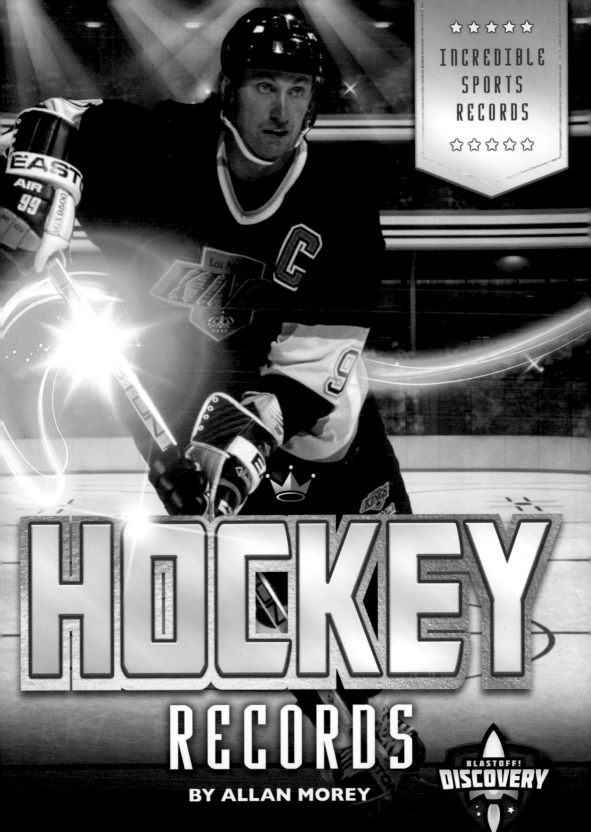

INCREDIBLE
SPORTS
RECORDS

HOCKEY
RECORDS

BY ALLAN MOREY

BLASTOFF!
DISCOVERY

Bellwether Media • Minneapolis, MN

Blastoff! Discovery launches
a new mission: reading to learn.
Filled with facts and features,
each book offers you an exciting
new world to explore!

This edition first published in 2018 by Bellwether Media, Inc.

Library of Congress Cataloging-in-Publication Data

Names: Morey, Allan, author.
Title: Hockey Records / by Allan Morey.
Description: Minneapolis, MN : Bellwether Media, Inc., 2018. |
    Series: Blastoff! Discovery. Incredible Sports Records | Includes
    bibliographical references and index. | Audience: Age 7-13. |
    Audience: Grade 3 to 8.
Identifiers: LCCN 2017032157 (print) |
    LCCN 2017032984 (ebook) | ISBN 9781626177840
    (hardcover : alk. paper) | ISBN 9781618913142 (pbk. : alk.
    paper) | ISBN 9781681034959 (ebook)
Subjects: LCSH: Hockey–Records–United States–Juvenile
    literature. |Hockey–Records–Canada–Juvenile literature. |
    National Hockey League–Juvenile literature.
Classification: LCC GV847.5 (ebook) | LCC GV847.5 .M67
    2018 (print) | DDC 796.962/640973–dc23
LC record available at https://lccn.loc.gov/2017032157

Editor: Nathan Sommer   Designer: Steve Porter

Printed in the United States of America, North Mankato, MN.

TABLE OF CONTENTS

RECORD SHOOTOUT GOAL

It is November 25, 2016. The close-fought game between the Edmonton Oilers and Arizona Coyotes ends in a tie. During the **shootout**, Coyotes **winger** Radim Vrbata takes the puck. He backhands it into the net. **Goal**! Vrbata just scored his record 43rd career shootout goal.

A GROWING LEAGUE

Since 1967, the NHL has grown from just 6 teams to 31. Most records noted are from after the league's expansion.

By the end of the season, Vrbata extended this record to 45 goals! His National Hockey League (NHL) record is one of many that have amazed fans over the years. Read on to learn about other incredible NHL records.

RECORD-BREAKING PLAYERS

NHL hockey is a fast-paced sport. Players speed across the ice while passing and shooting the puck. Star players have some unbelievable skills. They are some of the best players to ever lace up their skates!

In the NHL, **defensive** players do whatever they can to stop the other team from scoring. But **defender** Ray Bourque was also a scoring threat. His 410 career goals are the most ever by a defensive player!

REGULAR SEASON CAREER GOALS, DEFENSIVE PLAYER

Record: 410 goals
Record holder: Ray Bourque
Year record was set: 2000
Former record holder: Paul Coffey

Ray Bourque also holds the record for most assists by a defender with 1,169.

Many consider Wayne Gretzky to be the greatest player in NHL history. He could get the puck into the net better than anybody else. Gretzky scored an astounding 894 goals during his 21-year career!

REGULAR SEASON CAREER GOALS

Record: 894 goals
Record holder: Wayne Gretzky
Year record was set: 1999
Former record holder: Gordie Howe

Gretzky was just as skilled at helping teammates score as he was at scoring. He also holds the NHL record for most career **assists** with 1,963. Whether passing or shooting, Gretzky earned his nickname, "The Great One."

REGULAR SEASON CAREER ASSISTS

Record: 1,963 assists

Record holder: Wayne Gretzky

Year record was set: 1999

Former record holder: Gordie Howe

ULTIMATE RECORD HOLDER

Gretzky was an all-around amazing player. He holds 61 NHL records overall, more than any other player in history.

No other **goalie** has been able to win as much as Martin Brodeur. His skills at stopping the puck earned him 691 wins during his dominant career. The next closest goalie is more than 100 wins away from this record!

SUPER SAVER

Brodeur was one of the best goalies to ever play in the NHL. He made a record 28,928 saves during his career.

REGULAR SEASON GOALIE WINS

Record: 691 goalie wins
Record holder: Martin Brodeur
Year record was set: 2015
Former record holder: Patrick Roy

MOST SAVES, SINGLE-SEASON

Record: 2,303 saves
Record holder: Roberto Luongo
Year record was set: 2004
Former record holder: Felix Potvin

Roberto Luongo was another tough goalie to score against. His 2,303 **saves** during the 2003–2004 season set a single-season record. Luongo stopped 93 percent of the shots attempted against him that season!

RECORD-BREAKING TEAMS

While individual star players put up impressive numbers, how teams play together matters the most. With excellent teamwork and coaching, NHL teams can do more than just win games.

Few teams have been more commanding than the Montreal Canadiens. They took home the **Stanley Cup** 18 times from 1944 to 1979! In total, the Canadiens have won the NHL championship a record 23 times.

MOST STANLEY CUPS WON

Record: 23 Stanley Cups
Record holder: Montreal Canadiens
Year record was set: 1993
Former record holders:
Toronto Maple Leafs
and Detroit Red Wings

STANLEY CUP

The NHL's trophy is named after Lord Stanley of Preston. He served as governor general of Canada in the late 1800s.

The Detroit Red Wings of the 1995–1996 season were tough to beat. They won a record 62 games on their way to a Stanley Cup appearance that season. The team had one stretch of 13 games in a row without a loss!

MOST WINS IN A SEASON

Record: 62 wins
Record holder: Detroit Red Wings
Year record was set: 1996
Former record holder:
Montreal Canadiens

MOST SHOOTOUT WINS IN A SEASON

Record: 15 shootout wins
Record holder: Edmonton Oilers
Year record was set: 2008
Former record holder: Dallas Stars

SHOOTOUT LOSSES

The 2013–2014 New Jersey Devils had a rough time winning shootouts. They lost a record 13 of them that season!

The 2007–2008 Edmonton Oilers were an average team. But they excelled when it came to the high-pressure action of shootouts. That season, the Oilers had a record 15 shootout wins with only 4 losses.

The Pittsburgh Penguins had an impressive season in 1992–1993. They won 17 games in a row! This stretch set the record for the NHL's longest winning **streak**. The Penguins ended the season with 56 wins and a Stanley Cup appearance!

While the 1992–1993 Pittsburgh Penguins had a great season, the San Jose Sharks had a bad season in 1992–1993. They lost a record 71 games, including an ugly stretch of 17 losses in a row. It was their second year as a team, but the Sharks played like a bunch of **rookies**!

LOSING STREAKS

The 1974–1975 Washington Capitals set the record of losing 17 games in a row. It is a record they now share with the 1992–1993 San Jose Sharks.

MOST LOSSES IN A SEASON

Record: 71 losses
Record holder: San Jose Sharks
Year record was set: 1993
Former record holder:
Washington Capitals

LONGEST WINNING STREAK

Record: 17 games

Record holder: Pittsburgh Penguins

Year record was set: 1993

Former record holder:
New York Islanders

The Edmonton Oilers have been tough on opposing goalies. In the 1980s, they scored more than 400 goals in five different seasons. No other team has topped 400 goals even once! Their 446 goals during the 1983–1984 season remain an NHL record.

MOST GOALS BY A TEAM, SINGLE-SEASON

Record: 446 goals
Record holder: Edmonton Oilers
Year record was set: 1984
Former record holder:
Boston Bruins

The Toronto Maple Leafs have been in the NHL since its beginning. The franchise was founded alongside the league in 1917.

Only two active **franchises** have been in the NHL since it began in 1917. The Montreal Canadiens are actually older than the league itself. They were first established in 1909. This makes them the NHL's oldest active franchise!

OLDEST ACTIVE NHL FRANCHISE

Record holder: Montreal Canadiens
Year record was set: 1909
Former record holder: N/A

19

RECORD-BREAKING GAMES

A lot can happen in an NHL game's 60 minutes of play. Players do everything they can to keep the puck in their team's hands. Sometimes, this leads to unforgettable games.

The Oilers and Chicago Blackhawks played a game with nonstop action on December 11, 1985. They combined for a record 21 goals, with the Oilers taking the victory. This has only happened twice. In 1920, the Montreal Canadiens and Toronto St. Patricks also combined for 21 goals!

GOALS AND MORE GOALS

The 1920 Montreal Canadiens also scored a record 16 goals in a game against the Quebec Bulldogs.

MOST COMBINED GOALS, ONE GAME

Record: 21 goals

Record holders: Montreal Canadiens and Toronto St. Patricks (1920), Edmonton Oilers and Chicago Blackhawks (1985)

Year record was set: first set in 1920

Former record holders: Montreal Wanderers and Toronto Arenas

Sometimes fights happen during NHL games. On March 5, 2004, a brawl broke out between the Philadelphia Flyers and Ottawa Senators. Nearly every player was involved. A record 419 **penalty** minutes were handed out before this game ended!

THE PENALTY BOX

NHL players are penalized for committing fouls, such as tripping another player or fighting. They are then sent to the penalty box for two to ten minutes.

MOST PENALTY MINUTES IN A GAME

Record: 419 penalty minutes

Record holders: Philadelphia Flyers and Ottawa Senators

Year record was set: 2004

Former record holders: Boston Bruins and Minnesota North Stars

The NHL started breaking ties with shootouts during the 2005–2006 season. This put an end to ties in the league.

The Florida Panthers and Washington Capitals game seemed never-ending on December 16, 2014. The teams first tied in **regulation**. Then their shootout took 20 rounds to finish! The game lasted five rounds longer than the previous record.

LONGEST SHOOTOUT

Record: 20 rounds
Record holders: Florida Panthers and Washington Capitals
Year record was set: 2014
Former record holders: New York Rangers and Washington Capitals

NHL **playoff** games feature exciting action as teams try to reach the Stanley Cup. The Edmonton Oilers proved this against the Los Angeles Kings on April 9, 1987. They scored a playoff record 13 goals in a win against the Kings during this game!

MOST GOALS SCORED BY A TEAM IN A GAME, PLAYOFFS

Record: 13 goals
Record holder: Edmonton Oilers
Year record was set: 1987
Former record holders:
Montreal Canadiens (1944),
Edmonton Oilers (1985)

The San Jose Sharks took a whopping 59 shots against the Oilers on January 29, 2014. But Oilers goalie Ben Scrivens was up for the challenge. He stopped every single shot in the Oilers' 3–0 win! It set the NHL record for most saves in a **shutout** win.

MOST SAVES IN A SHUTOUT, REGULAR SEASON

Record: 59 saves
Record holder: Ben Scrivens
Year record was set: 2014
Former record holder: Mike Smith

RECORD-BREAKING PLAYS

Hockey is a speedy, action-packed game. Players try to get the puck down the ice as quickly as possible, often creating exciting experiences for fans. Some plays make the record books!

Scoring is not easy in the NHL. But on December 20, 1981, Winnipeg Jets player Doug Smail made it look simple! He scored a goal in the first five seconds of the game against the St. Louis Blues.

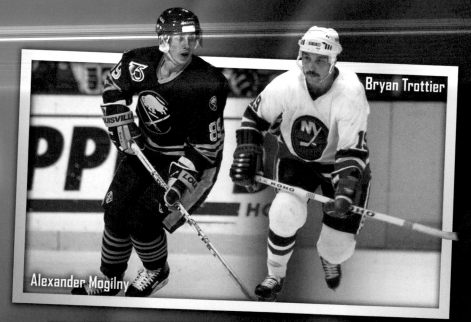

Bryan Trottier

Alexander Mogilny

SHARING THE RECORD

Two other players have matched Doug Smail's five-second score. Bryan Trottier did it in 1984, and Alexander Mogilny matched the record in 1991.

FASTEST GOAL TO START AN NHL GAME, REGULAR SEASON

Record: 5 seconds
Record holders: Doug Smail (1981),
Bryan Trottier (1984),
and Alexander Mogilny (1991)
Year record was set: first set in 1981
Former record holder: Henry Boucha

The Chicago Blackhawks could not keep up with the Minnesota Wild on January 21, 2004. First, Jim Dowd scored a goal for the Wild. His teammate Richard Park scored on an **empty net** three seconds later. They were the fastest back-to-back goals ever!

Jim Dowd

FASTEST BACK-TO-BACK GOALS SCORED, REGULAR SEASON

Record: 3 seconds

Record holders: Jim Dowd and Richard Park

Year record was set: 2004

Former record holder: Nels Stewart

Record: 108.8 miles
(175.1 kilometers) per hour
Record holder: Zdeno Chára
Year record was set: 2012
Former record holder:
broke his own record

The NHL holds a contest to see who has the hardest **slap shot** each year. During the 2012 contest, Zdeno Chára blasted the puck a record 108.8 miles (175.1 kilometers) per hour. This broke the record he had set just two years earlier!

GLOSSARY

assists—plays in which one player helps another player score by passing the puck to them

defender—a player whose job it is to keep the other team from scoring

defensive—protecting, as in players whose main focus is to stop the opposing team from scoring

empty net—a situation in which one team replaces its goalie with another player; teams might pull their goalie toward the end of the game if they are behind and need an extra player to score.

franchises—teams that are members of a professional sports league

goal—a score in hockey; players score goals by sending the puck into the other team's net.

goalie—a defensive player who defends their team's goal line

penalty—a punishment for breaking the rules in hockey

playoff—games played after the regular season is over; NHL playoff games determine which teams play for the Stanley Cup.

regulation—the normal amount of time a game lasts; professional hockey games consist of three 20-minute periods.

rookies—first-year players

saves—any time a goalie stops the puck from going into the net for a goal

shootout—a hockey tiebreaker in which both teams take turns trying to score a goal; shootouts last until one team scores a goal and the other misses.

shutout—a game in which the losing team does not score

slap shot—a hard shot in hockey

Stanley Cup—a trophy awarded to the team that wins the NHL championship

streak—a series of events that happen one right after the other

winger—an offensive player who mostly plays along the outer areas of the ice

TO LEARN MORE

AT THE LIBRARY

Frederick, Shane. *Hockey's Record Breakers*. North Mankato, Minn.:
Capstone Press, 2017.

Glave, Tom. *Incredible Hockey Records*. Mankato, Minn.: Childs World, 2016.

Hoena, Blake. *The Science of Hockey with Max Axiom, Super Scientist*.
North Mankato, Minn.: Capstone, 2016.

ON THE WEB

Learning more about hockey records
is as easy as 1, 2, 3.

1. Go to www.factsurfer.com.

2. Enter "hockey records" into the search box.

3. Click the "Surf" button and you will see a list of related web sites.

With factsurfer.com, finding more information is just a click away.

INDEX